The Most Controversial Book in the Entire Universe

IHSAN JONES

ISBN:0998513199
ISBN-13:9780998513195

DEDICATION

To my children, with love.

CONTENTS

1   ONE SOURCE   Pg 7

2   THE UNIVERSE   Pg 18

3   OTHER SPECIES   Pg 27

4   CONTACT   Pg 48

    ADDENDUM   Pg 57

    THE OS EXPLAINED

1 ONE SOURCE

One source is the inverse of a capacity to become
stretched outside of itself. The stretching is done to
perfection and once complete each inverse becomes
dominant. Each appearing as separate halves they
both have the ability to withstand pressures. They will
live within the containment but must come together
to become completely whole. The source will adapt to
its natural environment. This adaptation is a process
that occurs over time. The elements in the habitat
give the original source what it needs.

The Habitat

The habitat was made as part of a world for containment of the original spirits that are essence of the Source. The inhabitants can flourish but also meet their demise. In order to build the world, the cycle must be continuous. Catastrophes will occur and so will natural disasters. The outer bounds of the original source will be mirrored by its internal nature reflecting cyclical changes. We were prepared for our surroundings. The challenge was already built in us.

Each region has inhabitants indicative of its environment. The features and looks will be shaped by and are similar to the region. Influenced by surroundings, mouths will change shape and so will ears, eyes, and nose. Language will become a twist of fate as dialect is spoken directly by the tongue. Regional influence will make it appear as if the original source was altered when in fact it has remained the same. The outer stimuli of the worlds that change its appearance also directly affect interaction among inhabitants. Some will seem strange to others as their reflection is shown. These differences are minute tests of wills from the same original source. Like kind will affiliate but any kind can promulgate.

Many will see this as a separation, but the makers designed it to see a stretching of the original source. Many that stretched even further with looks and features that were influences of regional surroundings. The mouth would twist a certain way adapting and stretching further into the world that oblivion has taught us wisely not to forget. Our eyes saw the same things but in other ways. Regional influence became our only differences. Thus the original source was not altered but was formed to live in its own world.

The containment is purely an experiment of our Makers who are the watch keepers. They have invented the essence of time in which the old world spirits change direction to keep movement abound. They made up nefarious worlds in order for us to switch between them as soul keepers, watchers, and kinfolk. We are one and the same original source that's been altered by environmental circumstances. We don't get to choose our worlds until it's time to go back to become reinvented. Even then, the choice is limited and associated with our original surroundings.

Every living thing has its inverse. We may call it opposites. Every dying thing has its ability to reconnect to the original source. The soul is not lost on incidentals that are happenings that occur in the world. The soul is being trained to adapt and adopt

the ways of movement. Movement is what sustains

this environment. It has to continually refresh and

become anew.

Different Skins

Different shades are a result of a darker or warmer

atmosphere. Our hues are in a range of the elemental

earth. Our skin is shelter from those same elements

and our hearts are our shields. We have to be

protected. The Makers made it that way. They protect

us, we protect our world or what's in it until it is no

longer useful to us or the Makers. The Makers have

made the natural order to occur by default because it

to is an inverse of itself stretching far, wide and

deepened below. There are seemingly two worlds

within one (dark and light) but both are inverses of

itself and contain the same elements responding in a different way. One can handle its outer bounds, one can handle its inner bounds.

Whether we live or die is not up to us. That was already chosen. We must always go back to the original source to restart the cycle or process again. We never really die we never really live because living is so elusive that dying has already begun once we are sprung from our parts. The cycle continues with movement in time and motion as the gauge. We can remember parts of our prior cycle when we are reprocessed. Most of it fades as we move towards the light, where we get erased to start anew. It is a choice for the soul keeper at the interval of that reassessment of what to do. We will re-enter the habitat as a life form and maybe even start over as a baby. Resemblances of our old past have been erased. In modern times we will have lived as before but with

new adaptations. We could come back in any form

even as another creature. Buying time for the lifecycle

to rejuvenate is what the soul keeper does. That and

keeping the inner workings of the habitat fit for

consumption.

ONE SHELL

The shell that houses the body is in alignment with

the universal order. There are parts that coincide with

changes and fluctuations in climate, synergies, and

elements that make up the atmosphere within our

environment. The shell is hardened to be tough

enough to withstand pressures from outside. It

protects the most vital parts of our essence- that

which we share with all other things in the universe.

No matter what body we have or shape and form the

inner workings of our body are aligned with our mindset. We have the capability for self- healing,

What happened...

One source that inversed itself in every capacity. There is an opposite created of every cell. Each cell thus moves into form ready to master its systems. Those systems include identify of our true nature. We have yet to discover all the parts. Many have been identified but so many more are minute and subtle that seeing them can almost be impossible. Each elemental cell has a function for rest, movement, motion, silence, and stillness. Each function serves a purpose.

Once the inverse was created, there came from it multiple shades of the original version as we were placed in separate environments within the domains. Shades are a result of natural regional fluctuations in hair, eyes, nose, chin, and body parts. The physique is altered slightly as a result but the original source remains in human form.

These qualities became unique but as time advanced the structure and form from the original source created an alpha and omega. Each was a separate spawn that would require each other to reproduce. Two self- sustained entities that would multiply over and over by contributing its unique half. The genetic makeup flowed in the form of bodily fluids that carried future spawns for the next generations. Each generation would be replenished with multiple opportunities to connect. Each spawn would bring together half of the equation to self- sustain its own body. The fluids kept the original source living and were transferred as each opposite connection was made bringing its own half (the inverse) that would decide the continued species formation from that union.

How it works...

We live, we die, we eat, and we sleep. Our bodies are in constant rejuvenation cycles even in rest mode. We are working against time to beat it before our natural cycle runs out. We don't want to leave what we know behind us we want to propel it forward into the future where we will arrive again one day. It will be as a catcher's mitt, throwing the ball now and being on the other side to catch it. We have regenerated multiple times and the Makers will likely not falter in that plan. They take us, refuel us, reprogram us from the thoughts we think we had or from much of what we know, then they reinvent us as adapting from the original source. We may reenter as either side of the inverse, there is no set rule as to who we might be because we are already one and the same so both

sides don't matter because one is not better than the

other or has an advantage, it may only appear that

way in strength and wit.

PROCESSING

Processing occurs when we are called to our Makers

whom decide our fate with recurring options. We can

reenter while recovering-in that case we were not fully

taken and the choice was made to have us remain. We

can go along the path of erasure until everything

reminiscent has faded-at that point we can go to

either side, magnetic light or daybreak. Once we have

seen it we might be able to go back and talk about it

in limited capacity. Or we can be taken, halted,

interrupted abruptly.

2 THE UNIVERSE

One Source in the universe is the inverse of the world on its axis. It is a fine tuned shaped heavenly body that's derived from the source. The source as part of the heavens, is an orderly process with a succession of occurrences ruling the atmospheres. They rest within the hemisphere drawing form its dark side and light. God has revealed it as Jewels that the world thinks are hidden. This way our Makers, or watchers and our keepers remain at bay. Darkness shows their shadows until it is time to cross.

Star Gazers

We are star gazers ever wanting and yearning to get back to the original source. The Original Source is the supremeness that one seeks. That's why we draw inward for self- reflection. A reflection pool is ever beneath our feet. We drink it to fill or bodies and replenish our liquid assets. The gold mine that we house within ourselves are sacs of future babies. Future people that we will birth into existence. We carry one half of the whole and split the other half with our inverse. Our inverse is us- in reverse- carrying our other half. We equally can share in planting the nation. Our shades are what we inherit from the earth or atmosphere. We can live in the domain in which our bodies are adaptable. What we know about is earth and what we call heaven. Heaven is our original home. Our source of being masterfully created. Created with wise incision and precision to every detail. Our substance is matter of our Makers choice. It consists of nothing that we can make ourselves. We can duplicate cells because they are already being duplicated but we can't and haven't been able to originate the source.

Mindset

The most complicated thing that man can do is dupe ourselves into thinking that we are the original source. We are produced by the original source. Our way of doing things is because of how we are designed and fashioned. Some call it clay, dirt, or even essence. It is a multitude of substances that's magnified as we grow

and age. We cannot duplicate, reinvent, cultivate nor

agitate what the substance is. Our inquiries have been

left unanswered thus far. The molecules that we claim

are identifiable has interior substance that is not seen

because of its minuteness. The inward eye can only

imagine what that might be. The microscope tells one

story, and shows another. Complicated cells working

behind the scenes day and night as adrenaline pumps

to keep us agile, mobile, and having momentum. The

liquid nitrogen that propels us is as a faucet that never

turns off. The cells are always competing to generate

heat, energy, and thought processes. An interior

world of cellular beings housed within us to thrive as

if their our life depended on it. It's nice to know that

the machine (figuratively) functions on its own as

long as we feed it.

Life generates more life and the passage ways for life flow through our veins. The venues the cells travel to get to unknown places, are similar to the veins that thrive in the earth. Our earthly adventures are larger reflections of living entities marking and resting amongst the stars and planets. We are like the cells within the cells that can't be seen. To our makers we are fuel.

Yes. We are stargazers, ever wanting, and ever needing to be with our Gracious Hosts.

I have a marker in me. It is called DNA. You have a marker in you. It serves as a blueprint of each half that dominates from the reverse and inverse of the Original Source. DNA can be deceptive; one can have outward features of an inverse but inward traits of a reverse host. The two can complicate the process in many ways. Even the shade doesn't make a difference when adding to the mix.

We are not complete without the opposite happening
to us all the time. That is the duplicity of our nature.

Blue eyes- originates from cold cycle (ice, snow, blue
waters)

Green eyes- originates from roots deep within where
the green grass sprouts above the earth

Brown and hazel eyes- originates from soil, sand
dunes, and desert

Gray eyes- originates from evening gray skies before
twilight

Yellow eyes- originates from dawn sun rising

Red eyes- originates from a hot fiery source

Shades- Black, Dark brown, cocoa brown, reddish
brown, caramel brown, light brown, tan, pink, pale,

white…

The spectrum is cyclical and replicates. There is no original starting color or shade, it is translucent.

That is also why our habitant is translucent in order for us to see its contents.

The Good, the Bad, and the Rest of Us

Evil is a nuance because the very meaning of it has implications. Evil can be looked at as a rival or opposite of good. The good in every one naturally occurs just as its inverse. Checks and bounds control our efforts to navigate it. When evil reigns it is as if the very heart has been torn out of the body. Or the heart doesn't exist in the person performing the act. Consequences of evil can be devastating. Fortunately the ability to recover is within us. Redeeming qualities are part of the intricacies of our nature. Justification

for evil has its twists with acts of faith. Faith can

override an evil act at any given moment. Faith in the

possibility that good still exists. The inverse of the

internal affairs of man and woman is the same as the

duplicity in nature.

There is good and those who strive to do "good" in

all things. Then there is bad that has influence over

what is good. The rest of us who don't rest their

laurels on good nor evil try to strike a balance

between the two knowing the "act" as it is performed

is a matter of perception. Most rely on intent to clear

up any deception about the two. If your intentions

are good when doing a kind deed then the charity of

the deed might be received as such but if the intent is

with malice then outwardly showing a good deed

might be faulty at best. You may not always detect

that deception is present therefor rendering a kind act null and void. You might be wondering who is judging. That depends on your perspective again. It will always be the Makers and God. God has full control over all things even when the intent is not shown. The act will be fully judged from the extent that it does harm. The full ramification of your deed will have a blossoming effect and find its way back to you, in that way, you are being judged. Recipients don't have the full power of pay back. Nor will they necessarily see it. It is a rendering of the soul in small spaces that are unbeknownst to man.

3 OTHER SPECIES

When we meet it is through the twinkling of an eye as

we cross paths. Although we cannot read minds, an

intuitive response is sparked by curiosity. We will

either fight or flight as instinct dictates. Each soul

must bear its own burdens whether a bird perched up high, a snake slithering down below, or a seafarer deep within the ocean. Our worlds are intertwined as we touch each other. We belong together as our stories will merge. The makers have complete control over the outcome as our curiosity draws us near.

Deep souls living in the earth can touch each other in ways that others cannot. As living breathing entities there is communion amongst the planets that align to host their guests. There are many guests and each has a distinct host that develop it in ways that are conducive for its life cycle. The life cycle will vary because the necessity for existing for longer times of some is negated by others. We can all co-exist as long as the makers deem it necessary. Many of us will pass throughout life without having ever seen the other. There is no need to acknowledge every creature because they will exist as an exclusive arrangement.

Species will congregate in hordes of camouflage that

is predictable. Their reclusive nature is self- survival.

To know yourself is to know any other species

because we share the same capacity to want to live or

die. Often, what occurs in nature regarding the

natural order of resistance is the ability of each

creature to have instinct towards what's unknown.

Relying on the "faith" principle to get us through

blind escapades. We have longing for the order and

control of our master's. Our makers are the master

creators of each and every species that has been

discovered as well as the ones that are fully hidden.

We don't have to have intercession, or a meeting of

the minds with each specimen we cross. There is

uniqueness in identifying the qualities that are similar.

Some will be friendly, some will see us as food and as

the inverse predicts, the reverse will also be true. We hunt, we kill, we eat, and we will live. Even if we pick a plant to eat we have cost it its life in order to sustain ours. Species are of like kind and thus come from the same worlds. The cosmos has revealed its capacity for hosting a multitude of creatures. Even in the habitat of estranged beings, we can live and survive.

Angelic Souls that are watching

Angelic souls watch and send intentional intervention. The intervention can be random, rapid and give immediate response to alter a course. A person may not realize that this is happening outside of a normal occurrence but the recipient will know eventually that something has intervened to either save it or help it in a situation. Some will call it "good luck" or Divine intervention. In proper perspective it is neither good nor bad. Situations can go both ways making it an

Angelic force of reckoning. Souls can be called, lives can be ruined or saved. If the chosen is to be taken, then a marker is set at the last place of intervention. Mourning will substitute where the marker is left. A gathering of Souls for remembrance will deem the marker special. It will be where the soul was intertwined with another. The body has left to return at its entry when it makes its exit. One will leave, another will return. The form is which that life exists will have a permanent fixture (marker) by which to be known so that others can identify their affiliation with the person having left this earth. The Angelic forces stir a reckoning of the souls because they all are gathered before God. Angelic Souls are receptors or receivers of those entering. They are tasked with waiting for the opportune time to intervene. It is nice to know that of our own account, we were the ones doing the saving, when it's through direct contact with an Angel, seen or unseen that this event occurs. Most take place without us even knowing. A car can swerve from hitting us at the last minute, or we can somehow majestically brace ourselves from a potentially devastating fall. These examples of grace are moments of angelic forces placing us out of, or in some cases, in harm's way.

Much of what we know was ALREADY KNOWN BEFORE.

We changed the script to make it more comfortable to understand. There are as many doctrines as there are dialects and as many forms of belief's as there are species.

The Makers of the original source have made us to always want to come back but not to worship them but more of a reverence. A reverence of how pure,

simple, and complex we are made. Pure in essence,
simple if form, complex in design. Acknowledging the
Makers of the Source is respect for where we've come
from.

The entire body is a system that's housed and
protected. It's obvious that our makers love us and
have given us the capacity to love. We can also hate as
our inverse dictates. The five seconds of cruelty that
we succumb to when our bodies are deflated of its life
sustaining properties are not lost upon our makers.
They recognize that we must leave our present shell
in order to be processed and reentered. Cruelty can
sometimes be an act of charity.

THE MAKERS

The Makers have a neutrality that we cannot fathom.

Dying to us is the worst of what we can do. Dying to them is a way to bring the soul back home. We must be processed, there is no way around it. Processing ensures our continuation. If you look at processing as a readying or preparation, then from the perspective of our Makers we are simply coming home and not ending a life but shedding a body to be drawn back to that which nature has forged. Makers are our guardians. They watch over us, guide us, and intervene. They answer to a hierarchy. We have for eons existed through our Makers. They pass on the seeds to us to plant in each life. They give us leniency as to what we want to be, who we can intervene on behalf of while in purgatory or penance and choices as to what we might become when we return. Makers are Beings who can reveal themselves in light or dark. They are familiar with us and eagerly await our reception in the shadows or dark places that protect

them from revealing their true nature because of the

separation. A separation of both worlds exist so we

can only see their silhouettes or other forms which in

many ways are similar to ours. But there is also

something different about them because we are not

shown their full form even when they intervene.

Why is Dying foreign to us?

Let's face it. We reject dying. It is a part of us that we

have no control over. Yes, we can take a life, even our

own, but dying leaves a void and a quiet space where

there is no noise or movement. If we are to lie still

until eternity with all of our natural elements

returning to the earth, then that is foreign to us. We

cannot die then choose to live it is the other way

around.

The Angels of death stalk the earth to reap souls to reunite them with love ones, lost ones, and those we are affiliated with in some sort of way. It is not likely that we get to choose who we will see when we die because those that have already departed may be in a different state of existence. We may not find them among the stars at the time when we do enter. They may have a mission that is not connected. They may be in a holding state or have transitioned on to become something else that is temporary until they are called again. We do not all occupy the consortium at the same time even when we have died but we will go through the same processing as everybody else. There are those who will be waiting and may always have been. Their mission is complete in life and therefore they reside among the stars. After death there is a consortium of ethereal Angelic beings that

can shadow us and make a showing at any time. They

can pop in and out through worlds. Traveling through

space, neither time, nor sequences does anything to

inhibit the movement of Angels. Angels must ask

permission. Permission from the head or leader of the

consortium is sought before rendering any souls.

Allegiance of the Angels is to an important figure that

has to do with the original source- that which

originates the entire process. God is at the head of the

hierarchy and consortiums gather at the opening or

entrance where you are taken. It is important for

angels to be a part of the "Taking". The Consortium

arrives in a ship that is a gateway of transport. The

ship hovers and makes noise similar to having roamed

in space. It is a shuttle to the master domain where

the processing is done. When you die you will have

been readied for the process. Blanked out in time and space, the mind is cleansed. A whiteness appears because it reduces the shadows. It gets brighter as you are led down a corridor in suspended motion unaware of the state you're in. Those responsible for caring for your body will gently whisk you away. Your body will be present but your mind won't. Special care is taken when leading you that you are in a robe or white gown. Like a babe, you will enter a kingdom, floating and leaving what's behind.

SPIRITUAL LIGHT

The mind can exist without the body because thoughts can be harnessed. Corralled in space and transported through atmospheric synapses that touch us. Some of those thoughts will stand the test of time and some we can see through pen and paper. Each thought that is spoken or written can be captured. It is as if passing through a beam. There are spirits that protect the channels as each frequency passes. As spiritual elements, they have the capability to conceal or reveal any message delivered within them. A message in a bottle can last for centuries and arrive at the right time. A piece of paper or cloth can hold ink for decades. A well that's dug deep enough can echo the sounds of cries and laughter while shouts in a caves can resonate off of walls. The carved stones leave marks and books that are written can be treasured for all times. Those captured moments are expose' of the world. They give us hope that all is not lost since it can be found, captured, and decoded to supersede language barriers. The Spiritual light makes it known that everything that lies beneath or above can be uncovered.

TRANSITION

We can understand transition as not just an out of body experience or something that happens only when we are taken because everything is situational. We may not understand all the reasons while we live but we must take part in the transition. To transition is knowing that there are missed opportunities for growth and development. The source is within us so therefore connecting to it through transition will always have consequences. That the inverse is always possible is what we should understand. A person can act differently if they choose. Being "gay" as it is called in modern day, is a conscious choice rendered by the flesh. It is not an anomaly. The flesh responds

to inner workings that are beneath the surface. Our

conscious dictates what happens when we are pulled

in opposite directions. To some it is a calling. For

others it may not suit them to want to change. The

yearning (to belong to the other side) is a natural

instinct and part of our ability to connect to the

original source. Many people will take offense to

having different persona's when you weren't born

that way. But different personalities happen all the

time. We take on attributes of many people of those

that influence us. The attributes can take us in one

direction or another. Male and female can be the

influence. Yearning for opposites is normal. It is the

two halves wanting to become whole. Striving to

complete oneself by fulfilling destiny's challenge

makes transitional pursuits difficult. Being born in

reverse but choosing to be the opposite is like having the choice of whether to live or die.

Transitional pursuits are dictated as esoteric sequence or patterns that are complex in nature to transform the flesh. The flesh stays pure while transitioning even when altered. Everything yearns for the other half, even if that's what they want to be.

ACCEPTANCE

Acceptance is a ritual. It is entirely up to the individual whether they want to accept another person or not. Accepting the person is also accepting their actions. We can repeat acceptance rituals until our hearts content by qualifying a person under our own criteria of what is acceptable. You can be consumed by phobias that inhibit the ability to see past potential flaws. Flaws are defined by our rules of

acceptance. There is no right or wrong to acceptance
but there is risk, which is the possibility of rejection.
A great predefinition for acceptance is tolerance.
Acceptance by those that are not alike requires
tolerance. A powerful statement is-to prayerfully
respect (accept) a person's right to contact the source
by their rituals of faith.

Ig*Nor*it*

The ignorance applied to dissing someone is subject
to debate. Usually it is because of the "shades" or
"hues" of people. A person's color (that's dictated by
the environment) should have nothing to do with
how you would treat them. There is a lot of prejudice
due to differences in skin tone, hair texture, eye color
etc. Most of what we object to does not tend to
offend us- it is more likely because we see it as

different from our own enough to justify behaving offensively because of it.

A way to heal the process that causes unwarranted hate or repugnant reactions is to ig*nor*it. Ignorant behavior is indicative of not understanding why we must and should get along. It is not just tolerance for differences that we should have, but also a mindset that allows us to see past differences. Once we realize that they are not differences but enhancements that reflect our past and future, beginning the process to ig*nor*it (a derivative of the word ignorant) will begin the healing of lost souls. We can begin to find ourselves again from the enhancements that God gave us. Each of us has a past that we've brought along the trail. That trail leads us to many regions that will fulfill our purpose of grasping the knowledge of the various enhancements we will have on display. We

should have fanfare for the many cultural displays
that are present. A universal celebration that
acknowledges the natural order of everything present.
Cultural ties are relevant because they show affiliation.
Affiliated ties are also a means of self-expression.
Unwarranted behavior that indicates superior
indifferences in attitudes has no lasting place in
progressing societies. The inverse will always be from
the original source and shades (cultural norms, values,
hues), will be an enhancement. From the perspective
of the good, the bad, and the rest of us-love has
nothing to do with it. It is acceptance of knowing
who you are and where you have originated.

Why we lose our faith in the midst of our trials

"Don't shoot the messenger, blame it on the message". The cross bearer is someone that takes on all the burdens. They stretch themselves thin worrying about or carrying the loads of others. Wiping the slate clean is not enough. Often times we want to purge the body and soul.

You can pray for people to have comfort and become healed from their wounds. An active role is to participate in the healing process. There is circumstantial evidence that life is predictable and unpredictable. In either case, everything that happens has its aftermath. Trials and errors are unavoidable because life will throw at you needles and curves. You may not always see what's coming around the bend but you may get the opportunity to fend it off. Sticky situations can perplex you enough to make you want to run and hide. But sticking your head in the sand to act as if you'll never see or have problems doesn't

make them go away. Sometimes you have to meet a

situation head on. This is when the headlights hit the

road in the middle of night. Often blindsided, you

must act accordingly deciding the best option for the

obstacle you are faced with. A test of time, a test of

wills, each can be overcome with true faith. The

strong convictions in what you believe will have direct

effect on an outcome when you have carefully chosen

your course of action. You must also decide if there's

trouble with the message or the messenger. In that

case it can be either delivery or content. You don't

always get to choose your battles from what's

presented. Some challenges will be overwhelming to

the point of no return in which case we must find a

way to prod ourselves back to a rational starting

point. If everything is erased as if it never took place,

then perhaps there would be no memory of any likely

mishaps. But erasure is only done if memory is truly

lost and not just forgotten. True erasure to become

blank is done at the entry gates. For any faith that can

be shaken this would be solace for those that believe.

CONTACT

Much has been written about the contacts with alien

life forms. Folks have witnessed spacecraft with aliens

landing in strange places. These stories are being

corroborated by the recent contacts I've had. I

couldn't speak about the most controversial book in

the entire universe unless it included aliens. Sightings

have been happening for years with people telling

wild inexplicable tales. The outlandish stories were

not lost on ears and eyes of folks that have had

similar experiences. I for one was the last to believe

such tales, writing them off as a hoax. I knew there

could perhaps be something residing on other planets
but what that something was, left me clueless.

Perplexed to this day by the contact I've had, I too
am among those whose stories are yet to explain.
Some will see this as an attempt to extract the essence
of time by coincidentally seeing things that have been
talked about before. But this is confirmation that not
only do those stories exist but also the aliens. There
are larger than life entities that can contact us at their
convenience and not necessarily ours. Not little green
men with horns like some have seen but with
elongated bodies stretched above the average ceilings
that you and I can't reach. The height of the alien I
witnessed was enormous. Dressed impeccably in
woman's clothing the hair was flawless. The hair was
golden and worn in a bob that cropped the face. It
walked with feminine attributes. Wearing maybe

pearls, earrings, camel wool pants and a cashmere sweater. This is the sight I was shown when the alien was in my presence. I often wonder if Androgynous was more accurate since the facial features weren't quite as obvious. There was a deeply hued skin tone that was golden or caramel. The tanned skin could be viewed extending from the sleeve. The hands reached out for its target (which wasn't me). It grabbed the hand of the person to my right. The person it was taking was someone I knew. It also could have been a reflection of myself in the knee length white nightgown I had recently bought. It floated past myself headed towards the androgynous figure. Suspended as if it had been placed there to be collected and received. There were no words exchanged as the tall alien life form reached past me to take the hand of the lady. She turned around and headed back in the direction from which she came.

Right before exiting (or disappearing into the recesses

of the dimmed lighting that was prominent

throughout the ship, she turned her head around and

flashed her face looking at me for a brief second. I

saw a darkened or hollowed face as a shadowy

silhouette of what appeared to be features that I could

somewhat recognize. The eyes were recluse eyes and

there appeared to be scales on a skeletal formation.

Either the eyes were missing or deeply set so as not to

be seen. The flashing told me that it wanted me to

know what it was. It was an attempt at satisfying my

curiosity. I stood firmly and erect the entire time at

the back entrance in a faded background after having

arrived there from the light. The room I was in before

was facing it and as I stepped through the door the

next room had darkened. It was as if a transition was

taking place in a large spacecraft that was hovering. A voice spoke to me although it was telepathic and said, "You're in the bowels of the ship". The entryway did seem to be at the tail end as if it would have taken awhile for someone to walk there. And as the figure headed towards me I could see her turning from around a corridor of what seemed to be a bigger part. Before she reached me and as she approached, I had also witnessed a person to my right. It was a lady that appeared to be floating in mid-air headed towards the figure. She had a blank stare on her face as if not being conscious. Her head was erect and arms to her side while moving forward. It was as if she was waiting for something while in suspended animation. She was being prepared for something. I was frozen and didn't move while this event was taking place. When the alien got closer it was annoyed at my presence and made gestures while steadily walking.

Maybe I wasn't' supposed to be there. It could be that

this was a private moment I wasn't supposed to see.

In retrospect I felt that I could have been witnessing

myself since the white gown looked familiar but it

definitely was someone I knew, someone I felt had

ties to me. There was a seductive feeling about the

space I was standing in. An ambience in the

atmosphere that may have had a special meaning. The

carpet on the floor was neatly tucked and decorated.

There were high beams throughout holding up the

place. I couldn't see how far they extended but could

tell it was spacious. I also could tell it was in an

encapsulated portion of something much bigger; it

felt like a hub. The alien had traveled down a

corridor to get to the lady and entered by turning

from behind a corner. Although perturbed with me

she treated the woman she was taking with her with dignity and respect. She held her hand graciously as if the lady was special.

My eyes were wide open the entire time.

The experiences I have had were isolated but I was always able to tell someone by not being too afraid to speak up. There were other incidents but these were the beginnings of a phenomenal awakening that only angels can navigate you through. I was to receive many blessing after that

INSIGHT

The knowledge contained in this book was from experiences and telepathic inquiries that were answered from Angelic forces. The Angels not only protect me but send messages of clarity regarding the Original Source. Angels are our Makers, Watchers and keepers who answer to the most high. The highest

force in our entire sphere of reckoning acknowledges

that creatures must answer when they are called. The

promises of living forever (that's written in many

books) were already given to creatures of the

origination. We will continue to grow, adapt, and

prosper, under the auspices of what our Makers deem

is essential for us to be.

The destructive ways in which we sometimes operate

are a result of the inverse or opposites having conflict.

It is already deemed necessary that the two parts have

to come together to make a whole, however, being

opposite also causes collision. That collision may not

always make a cohesive match. And when it doesn't

mankind and creatures of many sorts will often suffer

as a result. The world can be destroyed and start

anew. Creatures (including plants and animals) will be

rebirthed into an oblivious setting which they know nothing about. As newly formed babes having to inhabit the world, their adventures will be plentiful and guided by our Makers. The process is to replenish. Shades will form again because there cannot be -one. If there ever was to be one again, the inverse would go back into itself and become self-sustained.

If you have had contact with an angelic force, acknowledge it, because it might be your greatest ally.

■■■

END

ADDENDUM

THE OS EXPLAINED

Well, it's good to know we aren't out here alone.

Right?

So how does it feel to know about the Inverse?

You know, a derivative of the equation of the

Original or One Source.

Feels great!

So what do you know different about the equation

that you didn't know before?

That as we multiply we continue to increase our awareness.

EQUATION

A true paradigm that influence the way we interact.

OS

The split of the atom of life. A burst of nucleus infusion that draws from its atmosphere utilizing energy sources as fuel.

Who made the equation and where does the OS come from?

There is no outside stimulus that can answer it.

The thoughts that transition through our brain cells
yield the entire complexity of the problem and as with
any equation the solution is twofold and has more
than one outcome.

You can ask, what about like kind or kindred spirits?

They all have arrived from the OS.

Why are not the sources plural? How is it connected
to this oneness concept?

There is oneness in true nature but also in pure form.
The OS has a mass attached to it that is adaptive. The
mass plays out superficially as an alien -foreign to its
environment. It is with- homeostasis that it becomes
familiar. Homeopathic remedies flush through its
flesh seeking correctness, wholeness and oneness.

That's why we are similar in forms and eclectic by
design.

The minuteness of our structure is akin to nature. The exploratory ramifications that are set make up our boundaries and individual fortitude. Each derivative must hold its own or perish. Even in perishing we multiply.

Why is this important?

Because knowing it-knowing the answers can rid yourself of the disease. The disease of always wanting to dissect what's already been split apart. We will continue our love hate relationships as the inverse predicts. They will have equal footing as we continue.

Then what is the ultimate struggle? And some may ask… what is the purpose?

The purpose is to continue to remain whole as a part of the equation otherwise we perish and die and must start anew. Each time we start may or may or be connected to our previous state. We can live in various life forms in the flesh or in spirit.

The calling of our true nature is protected inside of the brain. The brain gives conditioned responses to stimuli that defeats conceptual awareness. We cannot know it all nor are we designed that way but we can expand the universal order to include surroundings that accommodate mass.

Our comfortable or uncomfortable environment is what we make it out to be. Sometimes intense, sometimes complacent. We can have it both ways at all times in any given moment.

Have you ever wondered how you are able to change order or perception?

It is all relative to the state of being that is specific to each of us.

We may think one way and become swayed to think another.

It is empirical evidence spawn from openness.

What about the outside forces?

The outside forces will remain outside but sometimes they interact with us to let us know they're there.

The door is a veil not to deceive but to protect. We know we are protected in the environment because we thrive. Once we are no longer then it was chosen to be that way.

If anyone has seen the maker(s) they can share it here:

If anyone has had contact, they can share it here:

There will be those who will continue to explore the directness of the Source and rightfully so since no adjudicated answer exists.

So what is the OS?

A cure for humanity

Understanding the nature and components of the

inverse will free you of this:

Prejudice

Racism

Sexism

Ageism

Etc.

How so?

Because knowing that we are all one and the same literally will ease the challenge of indifference.

Most of what we face is conditioned from the part that knows we have split.

We still have to come together to be duplicate thus creating another version of our atoms and cells. Many of us will enjoy bliss as a complete entity while most will derive it from hell-that inner space or hellish nature that spoils the inner child.

Notwithstanding internal forces that are sequential to nature we will fluctuate- becoming cyclical.

That means the forces from within (the protected territory) will respond to stimuli from without. We can also pick and choose which adaptive response

suits us for survival.

So put this in layman's terms and help me understand.

It's simple.

You are here because something put you here and

that something does not want to be completely

revealed while we are in our present state (human

flesh).

The revelation is as individual as the act of birth.

Therefor it is truly personal.

When you seek you shall find…in a containment of

all possibilities.

To cure yourself of hatred is to first recognize that

hatred as a symptom of the process.

It is not the process but a symptom of being ripped, torn or separated in an inverse fashion. The more isolated the cell as a separate entity the more prejudice as it becomes focused on self- survival.

Community comes from having familial ties.

The inverse separates, then duplicates, and replicates its cells.

The cells stay intact but as polar opposites in many respects.

This is what happens to the cells within the body as DNA remains steady as our markers to the OS.

There are pathways that leads backwards and forwards, yet we thrive. Reversal of anatomy is the first obvious sign of the inverse. Opposite connections are the second. Another major wave is indulgence. Both sides will engage in situations that pull them back together. It is a major ritual of the formation of man/womankind. We will seek our connection in the inverse but we also have self-containment in isolation which does not conflict with gratification.

The inverse must continue the species.

Born of the same makeup in its entirety, shades of the environment color us. Domestic affairs dictate who we become as individuals, communities, and societies. We are free to be born, free to choose who we will connect with and free to use our faculties at our behest when there are no constraints.

Most of us will be used in some form or fashion as we attempt to escape abuse.

ABOUT THE AUTHOR

Ihsan Jones resides in Northern California where she works in corporations and in starting new business ventures. She holds a Master of Science in Cybersecurity. As an entrepreneur, her passion has been to share her experiences to benefit others.

www.ingramcontent.com/pod-product-compliance
Lightning Source LLC
Chambersburg PA
CBHW021912040426
42447CB00007B/826